Child Abuse:
Bruises on the Inside

Child Abuse:
Bruises on the Inside
'My Toxic Parents,
Mental Abuse and
The Subconscious Mind'

By Chris Radford

Child Abuse:
Bruises on the Inside
'My Toxic Parents, Mental Abuse and
The Subconscious Mind'
By Chris Radford

First Published in August 2016
First Edition
Copyright © 2016 Chris Radford All Rights Reserved

Disclaimer:
This book is not a substitute for the
professional advice of physicians.

Table of Contents:

Author's Introduction:

I would never have said that my parents were abusive, but I certainly never felt loved by them, and I knew I could never be the real me when I was around them.

In an attempt to seem normal I would often tell people about where we lived, where we went on holiday and what my parents did for a living, but I always shied away from saying too much because I didn't even want to admit the truth to myself.

My father was a charismatic vicar and my mother was also very active in the church, as were many members of my family. We were very stereotypical of many people on our little street and of countless others in our Yorkshire mining village. But all throughout my time living at home, I was vaguely aware that my siblings were treated differently to the way I was, and I was often called some by both my parents.

As I grew up and began to form my own identity I started to realise that I had difficulty keeping friends and maintaining relationships. I began to isolate myself and shy away from company, preferring to be alone than in the company of others. I could see that my peers seemed comfortable around people their own age, being friendly and outgoing appeared to come naturally to them. Having friends was like some secret language that I could never comprehend. I began to wonder what was wrong with me and my mental state began to degrade.

Even though the warning signs were apparent I chose to ignore them. We can't generally view parents as intentional abusers, they are our protectors and guardians. It is easier to blame ourselves and imagine that we must be the ones to blame for the way we are treated, and under these circumstances we can grow up with a poor self image. It then becomes hard to believe that we could ever be loved, despite needing to feel love so very desperately. Our experiences have tainted the way we see ourselves and others, and it affects almost all our thoughts and beliefs and soon becomes part of our everyday life.

In this book I would like to share what I have learned about emotional abuse, and will be using my own experiences to illustrate the points. The initial purpose is to understand why this particular type of abuse is so damaging, and the impact it has on our mental development. I wanted to discover if it was possible to overcome our past and move forward from this damaged state, and develop into the confident self assured person we were always meant to be.

Though this book has this as an initial purpose, it also has a central character at its heart - and that person is you! Some of what you read may well resonate with aspects of your own childhood and your personal journey. If this is the case I hope that in sharing my own story it can help you in yours. Childhood trauma is a very personal thing, it is different for each person and the way an individual responds to it can also be unique. But it seems there are some patterns to be found in all the mess and madness, and perhaps therefore, a common approach to resolving it.

Recognising Emotional Abuse -

Crossing the Line:

Many people can associate with emotional abuse because it is a largely subjective subject. Most people lose their temper at some point with a demanding child. Parents need to set boundaries and let the child down if they don't teach their children right from wrong. It is inevitable that at some point the child will demand, and the parents will have to refuse those demands for a variety of reasons which could be financially related, against social norms or for safety concerns. At those times the child will feel a sense of injustice and may grow up to resent being denied the things they wanted. With this in mind, how do we know if we were the victim of emotional abuse rather than the recipient of basic parental discipline?

Physical and sexual abuse are somewhat easier to define. There are laws that protect all people from being victims of these sorts of physical crimes, and if you have been subjected to either of them you are far more likely to be aware of it, and able to identify your abuser as the person responsible. My personal experience of the latter was far less emotionally damaging than anything that was ever said by my parents to hurt me, but personal experiences will vary, as will the circumstances and severity of being physically violated.

Emotional abuse on the other hand is not so easy to classify and some amount of it can sometimes be unintentional, yet its damage can be deeply rooted, and change the course of the victim's life. To help identify a behaviour as emotional abuse it can be recognised by some of the following traits:

1) If an individual is being spoken to in a manner deliberately designed to humiliate or degrade them.

2) When an individual is singled out and regularly treated differently than their peers.

3) Subjecting an individual to behaviours where they are deliberately threatened or frightened.

4) Where an individual is neglected, especially as an act of punishment.

Patterns of Abuse:

Being the grey area that it is, 'intentional' emotional abuse is difficult to isolate from the odd occasional or accidental incident, but where patterns can be identified there is an indication of intent. I grew up with two siblings, and could see clearly defined differences in the way that I was being treated compared to the way they were.

At least once a week one or more of us would be punished and sent to our rooms, often in tears. Over the course of my time living under the parental roof one pattern was regularly repeated. Whenever my siblings were sent to their rooms, between five to ten minutes later my parents would go to them, tell them they loved them, and told them it was okay to leave their room and go back downstairs to play. This is an import step in reassuring the child that they are still loved, and it was always no more than ten minutes that they were left alone in their rooms following punishment.

When I was punished either individually or with one or both siblings and sent to my room I was never told I could leave it. Not once was I ever told I was allowed to leave my room or given any sort of reassurance.

Every time the pattern was the same, my siblings were told they were loved, that it was okay, that they were no longer mad with them, and it was okay to go back downstairs. Every time I was left alone in my room. Even when I was punished with my siblings, they would always get the all clear, but I never did.

At some point I would desperately need to use the toilet, and when I thought the coast was clear and it was safe to do so, I would quietly slip to the bathroom. Afterwards I would return back to my room, whilst my siblings who had been allowed to leave their rooms were happily playing downstairs and talking to my parents.

When tea was called I would leave my room and go to the kitchen to collect it, but my parents would look away when I entered the room. My presence was never acknowledged, so I took my tea up to my room and ate it in silence. This pattern lasted for as long as I could remember and it was always the same.

I would remain in my room for the rest of the day, and only halfway through the following day would I dare to quietly venture downstairs, hoping that enough time had passed and that it was now okay to do so. It was usually not until the following day after that when my parents would actually speak to me, or even acknowledge me. The deliberate blanking and the absence of the reassuring words following punishment were a constant indication that I was bad, or at the very least a disappointment, and that my siblings were better thought of than me.

For those who are an only child, it would be nearly impossible to draw a comparison like this. But where there are differences with the way they are disciplined compared to that of a sibling, especially in relation to the same incident, the differences can be very striking and painful for the victim to comprehend.

Verbal Abuse:

Parents that chastise their children by resorting to name calling and exercising cruel verbal criticism are potentially dealing a lifetime's worth of damage to the child. At this age, they are taking in and absorbing any clues that show them how to behave in their brand new world. They are essentially an information sponge, and everything they see and hear teaches them who they are, and how to respond to the people around them. By subjecting an impressionable mind to labels or derogatory names they are defining the child and telling them who and what they are.

Unlike physical or sexual abuse, a verbal attack is a purely psychological tactic used to demean or even humiliate the subject, it can even be used to accuse or apportion blame. When people outside the family unit expose the child to such behaviour, the child should know they can run to their parents for protection, until they reach an appropriate age when they are able to stand up for themselves.

When a child is denied this initial level of protection they will likely spend the rest of their lives in a constantly defensive state. They never learned that they were a person of value or have the confidence to assert their position as a confident human being whenever the need dictates.

Much the same as at home, my time in school was spent trying to draw as little attention to myself as possible to reduce the chances of receiving a verbal attack, but like many shy and retiring types this tactic only served to draw the unwanted attention of bullies who saw me as a soft target.

In my time at school I was regularly kicked, punched, spat on and head butted. I've never understood why head butting was a thing, but at my school it was. I was also one of the unfortunate few to suffer a broken nose by one of the playground thugs that used to aim for the victims face.

The way I was treated at school reinforced what I felt at home. Only in isolation did I feel safe from the mistreatment and harsh words of those around me.

The term 'sticks and stones may break my bones but names can never hurt me' is a lie. Words can hurt when their purpose is to trivialise or put down another person. Name calling, even in jest is merely abuse disguised as a joke.

Suppression:

Another damaging practice is when a child is deliberately suppressed into an emotionally weak position so the parent can dominate them by use of fear. Being subject to this treatment potentially teaches the child that it is futile to ever assert their position either now, or later in life. If a parent explodes into a psychotic rage and displays aggressive or intimidating behaviour, that sends the message that if you do not conform, you will be subjected to a tirade of verbal abuse and suppressed into a weak position until you submit.

If the child does attempt to defend themselves later in life, it is unlikely to be conducted in a controlled and measured response because they never had the opportunity to exercise this type of defence successfully, nor were they ever allowed to believe their opinions mattered.

For this reason I quickly grew up into someone who felt they could never say no, and susceptible to being taken advantage of. If I ever displayed the slightest hint of not being happy with complying to suggestions, I learned to anticipate physical or verbal abuse.

To avoid this situation, I quickly learned to always comply, and became addicted to approval. I was prepared to do anything to avoid aggressive outbursts and this put me in a very weak position and left me open to being taken advantage of by people with strong personalities or anyone with unrealistic expectations.

In the heat of the moment, there are probably very few people who have not delivered an angry outburst at some point in their lives. At these times it is normal for the person who lost their temper to apologise, for those who use their words to abuse, there is no apology. This is another indication that the abuser is deliberately victimising an individual and indicates a suspicious pattern to their behaviour. Further indicators can be when this only tends to happens in private, makes the victim feel confused, or when the words being used are an attempt to control.

Injustice:

Name calling, or even 'a look' can be threatening to someone who is emotionally weakened. The suppression can become so ingrained that the very expression on the parent's face is enough to cause acute anxiety. This act is not limited to the parental home, and can be projected across a room or in public at any time.

If the child doesn't even know why they are being shouted at, they are powerless to avoid punishment in the future by modifying their behaviour to keep themselves out of trouble. A child learns how to maintain a relationship by reward or punishment in the same way a cat or dog learns that if it does 'X' it gets shouted at, and if it does 'Y' it gets praise. Where there is no consistency this can be equally damaging by causing an anxiety that is produced by never knowing when punishment is coming, and that it can occur without warning.

There is a deep sense of injustice when punishment is received with no apparent reason, and some of my deepest ingrained memories were of being sent to my room for no reason I was aware of. Having to deal with abusive parents on your own with no one else to turn to is a traumatic experience, so I was resigned to accepting that this was the way things were, and that I was the problem, but I was never sure what the problem really was. Perhaps I would learn it in time, perhaps things would improve when I finally left the parental home and went out into the world and left the confusion behind me.

The Retreat:

Having my own room gave me a place to run to, a place where I could lock myself away from the abuse of my parents. It also gave me privacy to grieve in secret. It was here that I learned to silently cry myself to sleep, which was usually every other night. I often felt that I never really slept like everyone else did, that I simply exhausted myself to sleep from excessively anguishing about my situation and my poor prospects.

My most prized possession was my headphones and portable cassette player. With these I was able to listen to soothing music, close my eyes and transport myself to remote and distant shores. I could spend hours looking out to sea and find my own personal solace in the grey clouds and the rain. Whenever I closed my eyes I imaged dark ominous and foreboding skies, with dark rain clouds and a strong wind. It was as though the crashing waves and the stormy skies were a reflection of what I felt inside, and they were strangely comforting.

I would go for long walks alone or with the dog, but whenever I took the dog I got into trouble for taking her out for so long, even though she seemed to love the adventure every bit as much as I did. There were a series of flood defences or levees several miles from our home by way of winding farm tracks where I would spend most of my time outdoors. Here there were deep ponds surrounded by a pine forest, with long shaded paths that seemed to fade into the distance. No one ever came here, and It seemed so peaceful and quiet, it was idyllic. No one knew I was here, I was alone in my thoughts and it seemed like the perfect spot. I had found what I was looking for, this was the place I never wanted to leave, so it was here that I planned to end my life.

The Bad Memories -

The Ones We Keep Hidden:

One of the worst side effects of emotional abuse is the insidious way that it manifests itself into the victims mind. There is a very high likelihood that the victim will take the blame for the way they feel, and assume they feel bad because they themselves must be bad.

Were you given love unconditionally?

Was love only given if you behaved a particular way, or was it ever given at all?

Were you able to be open with your parents?

Certainly in my case I was never able to be open. Past experience had taught me to be tight lipped about my opinions, what type of music I listened to, what I could watch on television, what I was reading, even the toys I was able to play with.

Brainwashed:

There were times when I would come out of my shell and let my guard down, times when I thought it was safe to play and have fun with my siblings. I was never sure what I did, or what I said, but there were times when my parents would intervene, break us up and corner me in one of the rooms.

"Say you're silly!"

Why were they so angry? No matter how hard I think back to those times all I can ever recall was that the three of us were laughing and playing, then we would be stopped, and I would be told how silly I was. Never the other two, only me. I had to say that I was silly, but even then I would hesitate out of humiliation. If I refused, the slipper would be brought out and I would be threatened with it until I relented and repeated what they said.

This always seemed to happen when I was happy.

It wasn't enough that 'they' said the words, they had to make made 'me' say them too. It wasn't just that I was forced to say it, I believe it was the fact that this was reinforced with such anger on their part. That the extreme emotion of the experience cemented the words in my mind in such a profound way. For many years, if I made a mistake or let my guard down, I would silently repeat the phrase to myself, so it had now become ingrained in my subconscious.

As a young adult I got involved in a charity walk to raise money for the church. In the weeks leading up to the proper walk, some of the organisers decided to walk parts of the route as practice and I was pleased to be invited and go along. Those walks were some of my most treasured memories. The walks were light hearted and fun and many of us were speaking to one another for the first time despite all being members of our large church for many years. For the first time I felt that people liked me, and it was a real boost to my self confidence. Conversation was easy and my usual social awkwardness took a back seat as there was so much scenery to see and talk about on the way. We all laughed, had fun and just enjoyed each other's company and the big outdoors.

Then came the day of the proper walk, and we were joined by many other members of the congregation, including my parents. At the end of the walk we all returned to the car park after a great day, and began to say our goodbyes. I was with two of the other middle-aged walkers with whom I had been with most of the time. We were clearly very happy and pleased with how well the day had gone. It was then that I turned to see my parents. What shocked me the most was not the glaring look of anger on their faces, that I was used to, it was the fact that they continued to glare at me with the same expression even after they realised I had seen them. I immediately felt threatened and became withdrawn as I walked back to the car. The journey home was made in complete silence, and I had no idea why, but it killed dead the positive mood that I had allowed myself to feel.

Breaking Point:

Because emotional abuse from such a young age can give the victim a poor level of self esteem, when they ponder their future it can be difficult to see a life that is worth living, and leaving the parental home can seem like a scary prospect. One day they will have to go to work and have a boss, they will be forced into a position where every day they must work with people who will likely hate them, and subject them to more of the same bullying they experienced at home and school.

In their isolation the mind is occupied with depressing thoughts that last from morning till night. They are likely to wonder what the future holds for someone with such a terrible personality. They face the possibility their life will be a friendless, loveless and painful existence.

In the face of physical forms of abuse, the future is a clear one, escape their tormentor, but when the source of the torment is their own failed personality, unless they can change their ways to make people like them, the future appears very dark.

Attempts to modify their behaviour may have proven unsuccessful because the abuse they receive actually has nothing to do with their own actions, but everything to do with the abusers hatred of the child. So when they are subjected to abuse regardless of their behaviour, then feelings of an inability to change their life for the better are long gone. These people are your family, they are your guardians, these are the people who love you the most, they cannot be seen as the baddy, therefore it must be you.

I heard stories of people who had unsuccessfully attempted to end their lives, and I would not make the same mistake. This wasn't going to be a plea for help, I wanted to end my suffering for good. I had no intention of taking an overdose, passing out on the bedroom floor and being found in time to be rushed to the hospital, and saved with a stomach pump. I had a plan, I knew where I wanted to go, and I knew how I wanted to do it.

Suicidal Thoughts:

When someone is in such a low place for so long, suicide doesn't just seem like a choice to end the suffering, it seems like the only option. The pain outweighs every reason to go on and fight another day, and it's a type of pain that can be felt in the entire body, like being physically broken.

In those times these people need another person to help clarify exactly what they are feeling and often it only takes one small step to help ease the pain. Very often there is at least one small part of the person that wants to live. They are looking for a reason to go on, but are unable to find one. Sharing that pain with someone who will listen has a twofold benefit:

1) It helps them to make sense of their thoughts by verbalising them to someone else, who can relay the thoughts back. In this case two heads really are better than one, when their own ability to think is muddled, another calmer mind can sometimes help give a fresh

perspective. It allows the feelings to be expressed as words, so the person who is suffering can at least have some idea of what it is that they are feeling. Being able to identify the feelings goes a long way to seeing a way out of them.

2) Sharing the pain lessens the crushing weight of bearing the pain alone in silence, which can help tip the balance in favour of delaying their plans for just a little while longer. Very often, feeling suicidal is a temporary experience, even when going through a prolonged period of suffering, the times when the person actively wants to commit to the action of taking their life is usually intermittent.

Regularly topping road accidents, heart disease and cancer as the number one biggest killer of young men in the UK, suicide is rarely given the attention it deserves. Regular ad campaigns and health promotions are being funded on everything from heart attacks and strokes to drink driving and various types of cancer, but only when there is a high profile suicide does it ever seem to reach the evening news.

If you or someone you know has ever considered taking their own life, pick up the phone book and call a suicide prevention line. There are some that are open 24 hours a day with trained volunteers who will respect the caller's privacy and choice. They are waiting to hear from people who are facing their darkest thoughts, and will listen or talk as required and in the callers own time and pace. They are there when your friends are away or asleep, and you don't even have to give them your real name. Indeed, whatever concerns or worries you have, these hotlines are there to listen. It's worth bearing in mind that most callers are not suicidal. These phone lines are unbiased and the call is usually free of charge in most countries and the listeners are often trained by professional psychologists. Almost all of these lines are dependent upon kind volunteers who freely give their time to help people in their darkest moments.

The Darkest Hour:

The flood defences were miles away, with various paths that led into the forest. I suspected that my body would not be found for days. I knew there was certainly no chance anyone would find me till after the job was done, and I could not have chosen a more peaceful place to spend my final hours. I planned to take a two litre bottle from the cupboard, fill it with tap water and take all the pills in my collection until I could take no more.

I was a frequent visitor to the doctors, and over the past couple of years since I was able to go on my own. All the symptoms of my pain had been treated in isolation without getting to the root cause, and as a result I had amassed a small collection of prescription sleeping tablets, muscle relaxants, and painkillers. The bag where these were hidden was stuffed at the back of a clothes drawer where no one would ever find it. I was very proud of my little collection, it gave me a feeling of power to know that at any time I could end the pain, and now I was ready.

What concerned me was the lack of painkillers, I wanted at least a hundred, so I decided to pop down to the chemist to purchase some more. Nowadays it seems you can't buy them in packs larger than 12 or 16, but back then they were sold in boxes of 100 and I was sure that would be more than enough. That walk into the village was a surreal experience. In a strange way I felt a weight had been lifted from my shoulders now the decision had been made.

The chemist store assistant was so pleasant and friendly. It was such a contrast to how people usually spoke to me, even in a shop. She greeted me and politely explained what painkillers they had in stock. As she was serving me I remember thinking that she had no idea exactly what she was giving me when she took the box down from the shelf. She was handing me the tablets I was going to use to end my life.

The transaction felt like it happened in slow motion. She thanked me as I handed her the cash, then she passed me back the change. She had such a warm smile, her whole face was beaming. Why did she have to be so friendly? I tried not to look at her. My mother often used to say she was taking my photo so she always had a recent picture for my obituary, and that thought crossed my mind as the chemist passed me the box.

Would this lovely person see my photo in the local paper and recognise me? Would she remember that she gave me these pills and know that I died of an overdose? As she passed me the box I realised that I had to look at her, I really didn't want to but I thought that I should. She was being so nice.

I will always remember that smile, it's like a still photograph etched onto my brain. A snapshot in time where this lovely lady with the friendly face is holding out that white box and smiling at me. How would she feel if she saw my photo? It was just enough to knock me out of the intention, because for the briefest of moments, I thought that someone might be upset by seeing that I had died.

A simple smile and a friendly face was all that it took to stop me in my tracks and delay my plans. There wasn't much of me left in the mire I was living, but there was still a shred of consideration for the feelings of a complete stranger, and the chance meeting of someone so lovely gave me hope that nice people did exist.

This part of the story also brings home the simple fact that what can appear at first glance to be a seemingly mundane interaction with another person, could be the only non threatening conversation they have with another human being that day. Consider carefully the words you speak and the body language you use when you meet someone new. No matter how brief or uneventful it appears to be, you have no idea who they are or what they are going through, but more importantly what they have on their mind. You never know what the person that asks you for directions is planning on doing with the rest of their day, and whether the interaction they have with you might just shed enough light on them to get them through, and be a memory they will treasure forever.

The Villain:

One common tactic often employed by some abusers is the deliberate practice of making their victim look bad to everyone else. Put downs aside, there are other more creative ways to turn someone else into the villain, and even make themselves look good in the process.

Lies and gossip are expertly sandwiched between words of compassion and concern to cast doubt on someone's good character. There are even those that seem able to do this with comments that are so vague, it's possible to argue that they haven't actually said anything at all. Yet when that person's name is mentioned, with a few well timed facial expressions or negative sounding 'umms' and 'ahhs' they can assassinate anyone's reputation like a pro. And by refusing to say anymore, they make themselves look like a long suffering victim who silently bears a heavy cross. Worthy of both admiration and pity in one nice efficient little package.

I always used to wonder why my parents friends would say rude things to me in front of them. Why did my parents not say anything back to them, after all someone was being rude to their child while they were present?

I was often referred to as 'the black sheep' and spoken about as though I was not even in the room. It's little wonder that I had a distorted view of who I was and began to develop such a low self esteem.

My role was a clear one, but that didn't stop me from making vain attempts with good deeds to try and work my way to being liked by my parents and everyone else. Of course their option did not change, I was not able to show them that I was better than they thought I was. They needed me to be the black sheep that they said I was, and so the die was cast.

Fear and Humiliation:

Name calling is the most immature of all attacks, where the victim is given a label, either out of fun or to deliberately make them feel uncomfortable. Usually the name itself is silly and clearly not factually correct, but it does give some insight into how the one saying the name feels about the person to whom they are referring. Name calling strays into the realm of bullying when the names are being used to deliberately humiliate the victim.

It wasn't until I used to spend weekends at my friends house that I saw what a healthy family unit was meant to look like. I used to see my friends who were all so confident and sure of themselves.

I was regularly called 'antisocial' by my parents when I began to withdraw, and they had no shame in introducing me as 'the antisocial one' whenever my parents met anyone new.

I also had terrible trouble sleeping as a child, and some of my earliest memories were of being so afraid that I used to wet the bed. I was never sure exactly what I became afraid of, but I knew that I couldn't go to my parents for comfort and reassurance. I used to rock myself to sleep well into my growing years and I remember that it would take me an hour to so before I dared to close my eyes. I was never sure whether it was the dark I was afraid of or something else, but I know that my mother would sometimes walk up the stairs then into the room and just stood there in the dark and stare at me. I would close my eyes and pretend I was asleep, but she often wouldn't leave and just stand in the dark looking at me. If I opened my eyes she would say things like "yes I'm still here" or aggressively say "I'm still watching you", or "I can see you". Then she would leave the room and go back downstairs to watch the television with my father.

In this type of scenario it isn't just about the words that are spoken, or even the aggressive tone, it's the place setting that adds further damage. The bedroom at night is a place where you are meant to feel safe and secure. Any trauma that occurs in a place which is normally considered safe, strips away security and replaces it with fear.

I never used to leave the bed when I was put in it, I was always afraid to, but both my siblings would frequently get out of bed and wander downstairs. When they did this they were allowed to watch television with my parents and even have supper with them.

A parent has the power and responsibility to nurture or damage a child's mind. The idea of a parent is one who brings you up to learn right from wrong and be your own person. Humiliating a child is not only a very cowardly and terrible thing to do, it sends subliminal messages to their conscious mind about who they are and how other people see them. The child will then try to modify their behaviour around the abuse which means trying to second guess what the abuser will think of what they are doing and how they might respond to it, even when the abuser is not present. So even when the abuser is not around, the victim is thinking about what they are likely to get called, or how they are going to be treated when the abuser does appear.

To exercise power over an individual even when they are not physically present in the room is one of the most heinous crimes imaginable, and this type of damage can last well beyond childhood and into the adult years. It strips away all self esteem, and sets up deep rooted triggers later in life that freeze the victim when certain situations occur. It produces an unexplained and seemingly irrational fear that occasionally paralyze them without warning. It's painful, it's crippling, and worse still, it is deep rooted in their past.

Pillars of The Community:

Abusers of any kind are likely to maintain a certain level of pretence, either in an attempt to conceal their behaviour or to preserve their social standing and keep up appearances.

Perhaps in some way the victim still loves their parents and does not want to betray them, so they keep quiet about the abuse. When the child has moved away from the family home, lies can continue to be told, and the loyal silence of the child validates the untruths. Would anyone want to hear that the pillar of the community is not really what they appear to be? It would be easier to believe the child is the black sheep they have been told about for many years, who appears awkward and socially withdrawn in public. Easier to believe they are a problem child than shatter the illusion of the charismatic happy couple.

Considering whether to say anything at all or continue the silence is a difficult decision, and either option is fraught with consequences. The abusers are masters of pretence and when cornered can suddenly turn the tables and make excuses, or cleverly shift the blame back on the victim. They can even claim that they are the victim and pluck lies out of thin air, and instead of taking responsibility they can suddenly be the one everyone rallies behind, leaving the victim once again standing alone and looking like the bad person that everyone was always led to believe they were.

The image that the abusers present to the world is not the reality behind closed doors. When you as a child see this, you realise that no one would ever believe it so very often you remain silent in your suffering.

With emotional abuse there appears to be only one course of action that does not involve confrontation, and that is creating distance. Getting an abuser to admit their faults is almost always going to be impossible, because to admit their behaviour is wrong means to accept responsibility. Where there are patterns to the abuse and therefore a likelihood of deliberate victimisation, the abuser is unlikely to go down without a fight.

Furthermore, to expect a repeated victim to muster the strength to stand up for themselves can be a lot to ask. Trying to put an end to years of abuse in a controlled manner when the perpetrator decides to respond with more lies, abuse or put downs, can sometimes result in the victim exploding with years of pent up emotional energy that once again makes them look like a terrible human being. A typical response from an abuser who has no intention of accepting the damage they inflict is the 'you're just being too sensitive' put down. This sends a clear signal to the victim that once again they are the reason they feel bad, and it has nothing to do with the abuser. It is an insult, it incites a negative emotional response and can cause the victim to burst into tears, which plays into the hands of the abuser who seemingly has their statement validified by the explosive emotional response.

Being repeatedly pushed and remaining quiet in the face of abuse results in an internalisation of all the years of humiliation and undignified emotions. It is for this reason that the victim has been denied the development of social skills to stand up for themselves even in the best of times, so the ability to make a stand is often not an option. The only chance is likely to be an advocate who has witnessed what has happened and can act on the victims behalf.

Having been the victim of abuse, I now pay very close attention to the way that friends speak to their children in public. The warning signs are often there if you know what to look for. If you have been the victim of abuse (and if you are reading this book then I assume that you have been), you may also recognise the tell tale signs. If you do see jibes or public mockery I would like to encourage you to take a stand, and put your friend in their place. I am very pleased to say that to date I haven't seen any evidence of my friends doing this, but having once been on the receiving end of one public insult when a friend of my parents actually did stand up for me, it made a huge impression and is one that I won't ever forget. Nor will I forget the time when my mother made jokes about one of my nephews and the response she received in return from my Aunt, who was clearly protecting her child and not about to allow anyone to make fun of them. Even at a young age, that gave me the insight that not all children were subject to the same maltreatment by their parents, and that some people did stand up to such behaviour, and that on one occasion someone once came to my defence.

The Undeveloped Adult -

Messed up Relationships:

When children grow up learning not to trust anyone, they turn into adults who trust no one.

Growing up in an emotionally abusive environment can lead the victim to develop a number of self defeating behaviours when interacting with other people. What was learnt in the home is carried into the first relationships the child makes independent of the family group. The same critical and emotionally controlling attitude they can learn from their parents can sometimes be unintentionally relayed to any future potential relationships, or cause them to sabotage prospective friendships. The emotional damage can be so severe it can even affect how they respond to kindness.

Emotional Exhaustion:

Venturing out into the adult world when you are socially unequipped to deal with it can be a traumatic experience. Working as part of team when you have never been able to voice your opinion without it being thrown back in your face is a daily challenge. Each time someone disagrees or has their own opinion, the feeling of not being taken seriously because you are insignificant rises back to the surface. The constant fear of angry reprisals keeps the victim in a near constant state of withdrawal and with an inability to rationally take criticism.

This repression can eventually lead to a low mood, social isolation and eventually clinical depression.

The victim can be constantly fearful that people who know enough about them to form an opinion about who they are, are likely to reject them. It is likely that such a person is going to expect the worst of people based upon past experiences, with plenty of opportunities to be proven correct.

Just one year after leaving school and in a working environment, I was referred to the mental health team by my general practitioner who had been diagnosing a variety of physical symptoms which appeared to point towards nervous exhaustion. I didn't think any of this was stress related, because this way of thinking had always been with me, it was my default position and nothing had changed except I was now in paid employment instead of school.

When the first appointment letter for the clinic arrived at home it was opened by my father who then showed it to my mother. My parents had an interesting response to seeing this letter which was clearly from the mental health clinic to me, and was referred from a doctor who was a friend of my parents.

Their response was not one of concern. I was cornered in the kitchen and subjected to an angry and aggressive barrage of questions. There were repeated demands for an explanation in what appeared to be an attempt to intimidate me into providing an explanation. After all, they had no idea what I had said to the doctor and whether I had compromised their reputation. However, nothing was further from the truth, I would never have said anything to a friend of the family for fear of it getting back to my parents. However, it was one of the few times that I recall standing my ground in the face of a barrage of angry questions, and I remained tight lipped about the appointment, and what it was for. It was never spoken about again.

Counselling:

The counselling I received did not deal with the emotional abuse of my past. The counsellor taught me how to meditate to relieve stress and anxiety which diminished my physical symptoms and allowed me to continue working. She was patient, professional and very supportive. What I learned about meditation in her sessions became the foundation of my stress relief toolkit for the rest of my life. But it wasn't specifically what I needed to help me in the long term, despite it helping me immensely in the short term.

I suspect that despite giving clear indicators that the relationship with my parents was less than healthy, the counsellor was not able or willing to take on the topic of parental abuse.

I will touch again on the topic of therapy later in the book, because I believe it to be a valuable resource. Some therapists specialise in certain subjects such as marriage guidance, or sexual abuse and so choosing the right therapist is vitally important for long term success in any area where counselling is sought.

Social Skills:

I was especially suspicious of anyone who approached me in a friendly manner. It was almost an internal recoil reaction, a sense of fear where I would be unable to respond verbally. Someone would see me and smile, then make their way through the crowd and attempt in vain to start a conversation. The result was almost always the same, I would stutter, or say something that to me sounded like a silly response, and the person would simply turn around and walk away. I would often see some of them again, but I would almost never be approached a second time. I will never forget all those friendly smiles that would quickly change to a wide-eyed frown before the individual beat a hasty retreat, leaving me standing there wondering what I said wrong.

But the pain of this experience repeated over and over reinforces our belief that no one would want to know us and that there is something deeply wrong with who we are. It is far easier to save ourselves the pain and learn to retreat from society as often as possible. Many people retreat into online gaming and shun real relationships, where an indication of our social standing is linked to how many likes, followers or virtual friends we have.

It takes a rare individual to recognise acute shyness for what it is. These exceptional people are few and far between, the ones that keep trying to win us over despite our complete lack of social skills at that point. To these people we owe a great deal in helping us to get some idea that we are worth speaking to, and that for at least a brief moment we made a social connection with someone.

Even well meaning people may eventually realise we are just too messed up. They may even want to help us and try in vain, but there is a danger they will consider us too broken to fix and simply walk away, reinforcing the fear that we can never be loved and are probably destined to a lonely future devoid of meaningful relationships.

Walls and Triggers:

The damage done to a child when they learn how to form relationships forever changes how they perceive relationships to be and the rules that surround them. They have learnt all manner of self defeating attitudes due to the way they see themselves and everyone else. They grew up being judged by the ones they love, learning to fear and expecting love to be thrown in their faces without warning. Except they didn't accept that it was without warning, they learned to look very hard for the signs to try and avoid provoking their abusers, and this becomes hard wired into the mind. They become conditioned to look closely for any indication that someone might suddenly turn on them, emotionally wound or abandon them.

If someone has a strong belief system, they will automatically look for evidence that validates what they believe to be true. This can be so extreme that anything which doesn't match up with that belief is emphatically disregarded and not to be believed. So if someone tells us that we are attractive we don't believe it. If everything we have been taught to believe has told us that we are worthless, then one person trying to tell us otherwise hits our mental brick wall, because what they are saying cannot be believed, no matter how much we really need to hear it.

In some cases someone telling us something different can result in an internal backlash, as though something inside is fighting this false truth like a wild animal. The mind does not like to be proven wrong, and woe betide the person who tries to help us break down those walls even if they recognise and sympathise with our complex issues.

It is also possible that the damage can be so deep rooted that the former victim can't recall the specific memories that caused the damage, yet the damage exists all the same. Certain situations can subconsciously trigger one of these deep memories like a form of post traumatic stress. Confusing feelings can arise in these situations where the person will experience nightmares, sweating, shaking and a sense of fear that appears to come from apparently nowhere. These sensations rise to the surface and in acute cases can cause the sufferer to panic, become disorientated, and even faint from a sudden change in blood pressure or temporary pause in blood flow to the brain.

Triggers are different for each person in cause and intensity, as these past memories or just the feelings they give rise to are brought back to the surface. It can be especially worrying for someone if they don't understand what is happening or why, and can lead the sufferer to believe they have a serious illness or something physically wrong with them, which further compounds their anxiety.

I'm Okay:

A major obstacle to forming and maintaining meaningful relationships as an adult is the acknowledgement of having an abusive past and how it affects the present. An abusive past has stalled what should be the normal and healthy social development from child to adult. Depending upon when the trauma began, they will find themselves standing stationary and only part of the way down the emotional journey from infant to adulthood. Though some development can be made by observing social norms this can be a slow and exhausting process and is not the usual route taken to arrive at the desired destination.

There appear to be two ways that a person with memories of childhood trauma will attempt to deal with the memories, when their ability to process them exceeds their capability to cope. The first method is to block the memories to prevent recalling them into conscious memory, and the second involves replacing the memories with alternatives.

In the first method, the memories are repressed and unconsciously blocked. When the recall of the memory causes severe anxiety and stress, the mind will close off the memory to prevent further emotional trauma. The existence of repressed memories is disputed by some academics, but for victims of abuse it is often a commonly accepted fact, and many claim to have personal experience of this phenomenon.

In the second method, the memories are substituted with alternatives voluntarily. Instead of thinking about the abuse and the way it makes them feel, they think about something else to occupy the mind. This could include thinking of a positive thought which is related to the negative experience, which distracts the mind onto something which causes less anxiety.

In order to appear that everything was as normal as possible I know that I was guilty of pretence over the whole issue of my mental health. I wanted so desperately to fit in that I tried very hard to appear normal and happy, even though I knew I was slowly dying inside.

In this way I was able to at least appear semi normal, I talked about my childhood and occasionally about my parents. The issue I believe this caused was that I had developed a mindset that everything was okay and there was no problem to deal with. There was no acknowledgement of my past and how it affected my present state of mind. By effectively repressing the memories out of the conscious memory I had a great deal to hide. This appeared to have manifested itself in a number of seemingly antisocial behaviours such as an inability to make eye contact with the person I was speaking to. Making eye contact was an almost painful experience which I could not maintain for more than a second or two at most. Only on the very rare occasions when I was totally engrossed in the conversation did I naturally maintain eye contact, but the moment I realised it, the spell was broken, and I had to look away.

It was as though I had learned to be so closed that the mindset was spilling over into many other parts of my life.

Isolation Spiral:

Some people who have been very emotionally expressive in the early part of their lives have noticed that after a period of intense grief the ability to express emotions suddenly ceased. Being one of the people who identify with this condition I am aware that following many months of grieving every other night in silence, there came a day when I realised that no matter how angry or upset I got, I found it almost impossible to cry in order to express emotion. Relationship breakups, death of family members, none of these things now elicit the desire to shed a tear even to this day. Though I have not read anything to indicate it, I always suspected it was my brain that had decided to suddenly throw the off switch. It was very interesting to realise that many other people also identify with this situation, and usually it followed a period of extreme grief or psychological trauma. This situation made it very difficult for me to get close to anyone, or allow anyone to get close to me.

My inability to retain friendships was something that puzzled me, yet a number of friends had politely noted that I appeared distant and disconnected, and that conversation was difficult to maintain with me, in part because of my inability to look directly at the person I was taking to for more than one or two seconds. I now realise that I was a very closed and closeted individual. I had both consciously and subconsciously hidden so many parts of my inner self that almost nothing was given away in external feedback. To engage with anyone in conversation, you are constantly looking for visual or audio feedback that you are still in a two way transaction. Without this it can be very off putting, and at best creates a one sided conversation.

The inability to retain friends or take any relationship to any degree of depth began my slow but steady spiral into an isolationist state. I began to feel more comfortable in my own company than in the company of others, even beginning to feel anxious when meeting friends socially.

Breaking the Cycle:

Babies are not born bad, they soak up everything they see and hear and the experiences shape their personality. We learn to speak in the dialect of those around us and even when moving to other towns or countries our accent remains largely the same.

Our early memories are the ones that most shape the way we relate to the world around us, the way we converse with other people and the way we view and respond to life's little obstacles.

It helps to view the parents as adult children who were likely failed in some way themselves in their own development. And in some way that can help heal part of the hurt and the blame we place upon them as the architects of our own damaged mindsets.

Parents were once children too, but equally, we are each responsible for our own actions and behaviours as grown adults, and must take the responsibility to get counsel if we realise that something is wrong with the way we think and behave. This is especially important if we, the broken child, are now a parent in our own right. The cycle of abuse must be broken. We must take all of the hurt and pain and make use of every available resource to deal with our past and move forward. If not for our sake and those around us, then for the sake of our children.

Maintaining Parental Contact -

The Dysfunctional Family Unit:

In many cases the relationship with the abusive parents does not end when we fly the nest. Extended family, siblings and the desire for normality keep us attached to our family roots. It can be easy to imagine that things will be different when we ourselves become adults, that there is a sense of distance, that we can choose when and for how long we see our parents and that by limiting contact we can maintain a sense of family whilst keeping them at arm's length.

Maintaining Normality:

The surface relationship is one consideration. Over time a natural rhythm may develop of phone calls and brief visits where an equilibrium is reached that both parties become accustomed to. This was the case in my relationship to my parents when I left home. It took time to develop, but we would see one another two or three times a year and at Christmas, with phone calls every six to eight weeks. I would call them, or they would call me, and this maintained the relationship over a number of years.

Even when I moved further away, this pattern continued. There was a more or less equal number of calls made by me or my parents, where only neutral topics were discussed. The weather, what the rest of the family were doing, and other non threatening topics were the only ones ever covered.

My parents never asked me about my friends or why I was still single. I would occasionally talk about work, but nothing in too much detail, nor was I ever asked. As this new surface relationship with my parents was maintained over fifteen years, the boundaries were self evident. It never strayed, nor did it ever broaden into something deeper. The only noticeable change was an absence of being invited over for Christmas after the first few years. Occasionally I was asked what I did over the holiday period, and the answer was the same 'I was not doing anything'.

It never seemed to bother them, but it did each year momentarily bother me that I would be told my siblings were spending Christmas with them, and that I now wasn't being invited.

Though it was clearly a rejection, I learned to make the most of it, and made my own plans for Christmas each year. I didn't allow myself to dwell on the matter because I knew that if I did stop to consider how I felt and what it might mean I would probably feel quite dejected. I needed to protect my own state of mind, occasionally that meant not asking myself how I felt about every indication that there was more wrong with the relationship than I dared believe.

I remember one year completely out of the blue when my parents came to stay, that my father suddenly asked me if I wanted to come down for the holiday. I was so shocked I immediately replied 'yes please' and spent the holiday time with them. I was sure to take a hamper of food, gifts, and help out where I could and I enjoyed my time with them. I left in a good frame of mind and was grateful for having had a normal family Christmas for once. But that was the last time I was ever invited. The following year my mother called to check 'that I wasn't coming down that year as they had invited friends who would be staying with them' instead. It was such a cold conversation on my mother's part, very clinical and matter of fact, but despite this set back, the regular pattern of phone calls continued, and I went back to my usual solitary Christmas routine.

Risks and Benefits:

In many ways it can help to heal the wounds of childhood if a semblance of a normal healthy parent child relationship can be maintained. Some people are unaware of their actions, and even if they are, they have no idea how destructive some of them can be. In this case, it is easier to eventually forgive and move on to enjoy the new relationship you have with your parents, but some people are so wounded they are unable to do this.

Often some relationship is better than nothing at all, and this might be especially true when the parents then become grandparents and you want your children to grow up knowing they have a granny and granddad. Depending upon the extent of the abuse, leaving children alone with them might not be prudent, but this is wholly situational.

In some cases the abuse continues to be directed at the victim even as an adult, but in a different way. Emotional abuse, unlike physical or sexual can be just as potent over the phone as it can be in person. Mind games, criticism and verbal abuse can now be delivered via email, text, video link or telephone. Online abuse is an ever growing concern amongst children, but some of the perpetrators can be much older, and can be known to their victims.

Certainly in my case the exclusions continued the same as they did while I was still living at home. Both my siblings were invited each Christmas and also to other events such as the renewal of my parents wedding vows, which I wasn't even aware of until after it had happened. In no conversation did they ever give any indication they were planning to do this, yet both my siblings had been invited and were present. My mother was never shy in cases like these of letting me know what had happened and who had been present, which usually meant everyone except me. Each time it felt like a dagger to the heart and continued the pattern of exclusion I had felt as a child. I will never know what reasons were given if people ever asked where I was, and why I hadn't been able to make it to these events. It was just another consideration that I learned to bury in order to maintain the surface relationship.

Exclusions:

One day I received a phone call from my mother at work. 'There's nothing to worry about, but your Gran has been rushed to hospital, there's no need to come down, I'm just letting you know I'm heading over there now'.

But I did want to go to the hospital, I was only round the corner and under the circumstances I knew my Manager would have no problem with it. But no, I was told again that there was no need, and this was repeated again twice in an ever firmer tone when I expressed a desire to go, then again quite aggressively. I backed down because I didn't want to upset her further. Clearly she was upset, this was her mother who had been rushed to the hospital, and perhaps she wanted time alone with her.

My Manager was sat opposite heard the whole conversation and said I should ignore what my mother had said and go to the hospital straight away. But I didn't want to risk a confrontation, so to put my mind at rest I called the hospital to see how my Gran was. She wasn't doing well and the Charge Nurse told me to come down straight away as she wasn't expected to last much longer. I shut down my computer, picked up my bag and called my mother to say I was on my way.

When I called my mother had already arrived and was clearly very angry that I had called the hospital. I told her I had shut down my computer, that my Manager had relieved me, I had my bag and was heading out the door and would see her in about ten minutes. This made her even more angry, and she told me again that there was no need for me to go down.

Obviously upset, and now slumped at my desk with my bag in my lap, my Manager said something that will always stick with me. That 'although it was her mother who had been rushed to hospital, it was also my Gran, and I had a right to be there'.

About half an hour later my brother called me to tell me that my Gran had died. He sounded upset, but he also sounded angry. I asked him if he was okay, but he simply made a point of saying that he was there at the hospital supporting mum and dad, and was with Gran when she died. I asked him if he had called my sister, and his response was simply that she was also at the hospital supporting mum and dad, and was with Gran when she died.

Breaking the Rules:

One day a number of years later, my father fell suddenly and unexpectedly ill. It was a long term medical condition which was going to shorten his life and leave him less mobile than he had previously been accustomed to. During this time there were many tests, scans, adjustments to medications and visits to the specialists. During this time, many were concerned for his health, and I was one of them.

Where before the phone calls had been every six weeks, they were now every week. Each week a new test, or visit to the specialist. I would call at the end of those days or the following day to get the latest news. This scenario went on for around two months as doctors tried to strike the right balance of drugs for maximum effect. It was at the end of this two months that the phone calls began being pre-empted by emails from my mother. In emails addressed specifically to me, she was letting me know the outcome of the tests and consultations. At first I was taken aback by the new method of communication. Not only was it outside the norm, it also seemed, at least to me, to be an inappropriate method of communication given the tone and seriousness of the news. I would usually type a reply, but for some of the emails I decided it was more appropriate to call instead. It didn't seem right to be emailing about something so serious, and an email seemed to trivialise the severity of the news.

It was clear that by phoning more frequently I had broken the unwritten rule that existed for so many years of only communicating every six weeks. I wasn't sure if my father was just tired, tired of talking about the condition or tired of talking to me. Sometimes it would be my mother who would give me the update when I called, but that was when the conversations took a turn for the worse.

I didn't want to believe that my increased number of calls was causing a problem. I assumed the way they were talking to me was due to concern about my father's health, but I now suspect that the emails were a method of trying to limit the amount of contact.

The telephone conversations began to get strange. On phone calls my mother started to interrupt me and repeat back my last sentence, but change some of the words. The first time this happened I wondered if I genuinely had said something different to what I intended, but on the subsequent phone calls I realised she was deliberately misquoting me for unknown reasons. To make matters worse, in order to keep the peace I assumed she simply misheard and when I repeated back what I 'thought I had said' she became aggressive and verbally abusive. This was a very confusing experience that I had never seen before. Why was I being misquoted on every phone call, and why was she now saying that I always did this?

On our final phone call it happened again, but this time the phone call was followed up with an email. I only managed to read the first two sentences. It was clear from those first few words what the tone for the rest of the email would be, and it wasn't until the following day that I felt able to read the rest.

Separation:

After trying to maintain a relationship with my parents for so many years, I would never have foreseen that they would be the ones to end the relationship, let alone to communicate this by email. It was clear that they were okay with occasional contact, but the illness of my father and the increased phone calls were enough for them to suggest we didn't speak to one another anymore. It validated all the feelings of rejection that I tried so hard to ignore since I was a child, it was hurtful, it was embarrassing and it was an insult. But I accepted it, and moved on.

What followed was six months of learning to live with what it meant to be truly rejected. I held out hope that they might contact me again and say they didn't mean it, but they never did. But after approximately six months a strange thing began to happen. I began to feel as though a weight had been lifted, and I felt as though it might actually work out for my best.

After I realised that some sort of healing was already beginning to take place I knew that even if they did contact, I would choose to keep them out of my life for the foreseeable future. After the shame of being rejected so very clearly, I finally felt that I was able to move forward, but what I didn't realise until a number of years later was that I needed to accept another truth before I could stand any chance of living a full life in the future, despite the separation.

Taking Back Control -

Breaking the Destructive Pattern:

Coming to terms with the past shame allows us to learn and understand ourselves better, and then move forward. It's difficult to separate the history of the childhood memories from who we are today if the architects of our pain are still present in our lives. But separation from our parents has emotional and social consequences and should never be taken lightly.

I would often speak of my past when socialising, choosing only the safe topics and steering clear of the bad. The issue I didn't notice until sometime after the separation, was that even when thinking or speaking of only the neutral aspects of the relationship with my parents, it meant, they were still very much in my thoughts. Just thinking about them at all caused me a certain degree of anxiety, which always led to the more sobering and painful memories. Deciding to not mention or even think about them decreased my anxiety even further, until in the end I just stopped talking about them altogether.

I saw the pattern and I decided to run with it. They were something I never talked about, so in turn I stopped thinking about them and this appeared to break a cycle of thought, and I felt a sense of progress was finally being made.

Living with the Consequences:

There are a number of things to consider when you decide to deal with your abusive past. Even if you decide to maintain a relationship with your parents, when you uncover painful memories and explore your current state of mind all the emotions can come pouring back out.

If you do decide to detach yourself, you need to be prepared to live with being ostracised by other family members, and not knowing what is being said behind your back. Think very carefully about separating yourself from them, deciding to keep them at arm's length and maintaining a basic relationship might be the best way to go. If they continue to be verbally and emotionally abusive your choice might be the inevitable conclusion of separation to protect yourself from further damage. Then there is the decision of whether to forgive and move on, or do both.

Separation is the last resort, but if the pain of meeting them and maintaining a relationship is greater than the pain of being apart, this might be another indicator of which might be right decision for you.

The choice is yours to make.

Consider if the current relationship is healthy and normal? How unhappy is it making you? Is the contact inhibiting your further development?

Ask yourself the following questions to help balance the argument, and write the answers down if it helps you to make sense of the pros and cons:

1. What is good about the relationship you have now?

2. Are there benefits to you emotionally by maintaining the relationship?

3. Does the current relationship provide you with any social stability, and in what way?

4. In their best moments, how have your parents shaped you, and does this outweigh the pain?

Taking the time to answer these few questions might help make the decision a little easier, but remember that not making a decision is always an option too, and so is putting the decision off to another day.

Another consequence to consider is how you will feel after the loss of contact when you don't know what people are saying about why you are not in contact with them anymore. This was the pain that I felt after my parents were the ones to separate themselves from me. I knew it was unlikely that they were going to tell the truth, as no parent who wishes to maintain their wholesome image would want to admit that they emailed their child to tell them they didn't want any more contact with them.

In my case sadly I did eventually find out what they were saying, and it was as I suspected. They claimed to not know what was happening, and that I had somehow fallen out with them for some unknown reason. In this case I consoled myself with the fact that if anyone cared about me heard this, they could always make the effort to contact me directly and ask me if I was okay. I remembered when I was younger they said a similar thing about other family members who we suddenly stopped visiting. As a child I occasionally used to ask why we never saw certain relatives anymore, and was told that they had fallen out with us but they didn't know why.

If you can live with the decision to cut them out of your life and move forward to recover your emotional development, then sleep on it for a couple of days and see if you still come to the same conclusion.

Dying with the Consequences:

Two years after the email some of the hurt still lingered. I had resigned myself to the fact that I would never fully get over that I had been rejected by people who traditionally never should do. I tried to make the best of it and made some amount of progress in healing the pain of my past.

One day my father passed away suddenly, but I was unaware of this. When someone asked if I knew, my mother told them that my phone number had changed, so there was no way to contact me. Of course my phone number hadn't changed and there was no reason to believe that it had.

A number of days passed by and they contacted their local police force to tell them there was no way to contact me, and could they break the news to me that my father had died. To be visited in the middle of the night by police officers, who have been used to relay a communication that could have been made by a relative with a simple phone call is somewhat embarrassing. It isn't a nice job for police to inform family members that a relative has died, and I must have apologised to them at least three or four times. They were really pleasant, and to be honest, they were probably more compassionate than my immediate family would ever have been.

I called my siblings that morning and spoke to my mother to offer my condolences. It was a short call, but I felt that I should at least let them know that I planned on going to the funeral. It seemed only right to do so.

By this time the funeral had been arranged and I had spoken to my brother who gave me the location and time of the service. I will never know why I felt the compulsion to go to the funeral of a man who had mentally abused and then abandoned me, but I wasn't sure if I would be able to live with myself if I didn't. As it was going to be a five hour journey, I had messaged my brother to confirm the time and place of the funeral and he responded to say he would see me there.

Not only was the funeral being held several miles away at a place with a completely different name, it was also half an hour later than the time he gave me.

Humiliation and confusion are two emotions that make very bad bedfellows, but on my way back home I made an important decision. I gave myself one day to grieve, and then I vowed to cut them out my life for good. I promised myself a future where I never thought about them, never concerned myself what other family members might be thinking, and that I would never even speak about any of them again.

Healing the Inner Child:

As time went by I took a unique approach to repairing the damage of my past, that proved quite successful. When you make the decision to reclaim your emotional wellbeing, you have the opportunity to take the role of a parent to your broken inner child. You can learn to give yourself unconditional love, never lose your temper and treat yourself with the loving kindness you deserve.

When you lose the car keys or misplace your glasses it is important to be slow to anger and quick to forgive. Learn to appreciate yourself and how to spend quality time alone being comfortable in your own skin.

You can give yourself all the attention that you desire, make time for yourself, and schedule in what a friend of mine likes to call 'me time'. You can devote the best parts of the day to your own growth and fulfilment, and give yourself attention and now put yourself first at least some of the time.

Learn how to make yours a happy house, make it the sort of caring loving home you would have wanted to grow up in, and consider some of the following strategies to show your inner child that it is significant and it matters:

Read: I find it both fascinating and encouraging that for all the toys and gadgets we have nowadays children still love to be read to. Choose reading material that will uplift and inspire you. If you need to read self-help books to help steer you in a positive direction, then purchase books that motivate you with titles that resonate with your ultimate goals. If you enjoy a good story but never seem to have the time to read, set the time aside, especially in the evening to curl up with a good book on the sofa and devote a good hour to lose yourself in the pages.

Relationships: The people that surrounded you as a child helped to shape you into the adult you are now. Choose your relationships carefully and remove the toxic people from your life, or keep them at arm's length while you heal. Negativity and oppression are to be avoided. Ask yourself if each of your relationships are healthy and add value to your life, or if they drain and sap your energy. Feel no compulsion to put other peoples interests above your own. Yes there are times when it is important to put others first, but ask yourself if you make a habit of doing this too often, and consider if you are out of balance.

Affirmations: If you find yourself saying that you're not good enough or you often think that you are unlovable then you need to deprogram the emotional damage of your past and change your innermost opinions about who you are and what you are about. Affirmations are a strange daily exercise to those who are new to them, it can almost seem like a haughty way to start the day. Telling yourself how good you are and how everything is going so well feels like telling yourself a lie, but it's for this very reason that you need affirmations to boost your self esteem and reprogram your mind until it becomes acceptable to believe that you are a person of worth and value.

Therapy: This can be really useful if you find you are still struggling to come to terms with what happened in your past and need professional counselling. Sometimes we don't know what we feel or what to think, but a good therapist will act as a blank canvas and help you to understand and make sense of your thoughts. They can help you to get to know yourself better and explore your past and present in a controlled and professional environment. Be sure not to be led by a therapist who is making suggestions whilst trying to help you uncover repressed memories. This could cause you to have a distorted view of what happened in your past, or believe that things happened to you that didn't. Remember you are in control, they are there to support your understanding and not interpret it for you. When you try to locate a good counsellor, ask them if they specialise in emotional abuse and childhood trauma.

Self help might not work for you as well as you would like. If that's the case get professional help.

Videos: What television programs and movies make you really happy? Remember children tend to spend a lot of time watching mindless cartoons and laughing at inane things on the television. Though I'm not suggesting that you sit in front of the television watching cartoons every night, you might want to consider watching uplifting mood boosting shows that you enjoy.

Also consider the fact that children don't generally speaking watch the news. They are largely oblivious to the all the national murders and the suffering in other countries. For a while at least, consider reducing the quantity of depressing programs for the ones that inspire or engage you in a positive way. Possibly restrict your news intake to the headlines only for a little while, and see how that works out for you.

Journaling: Instead of asking what is wrong with you, ask what is right with you, and good about your life. What is working for your benefit, and can you see a pattern in the days that you consider to be the really great ones. Asking yourself different questions can completely change your outlook on life and the direction it takes. See yourself as the very best you, imagine you are living the life you would really like and what that would look like. Write this down so you have a clear picture of your ideal life and decide today what you can do to take the first small step of making it a reality.

Write down what makes you happy, list all the good memories and how they made you feel. Know that you were this happy once before, and you can be again. Make a list of all the things that you would like to do and name a few of your life's big ambitions. Decide how to make one of those ambitions come true, and plan for it.

Meditation: The practice of guided meditation eases stress and anxiety and will dramatically improve your quality of life. The easiest for beginners to try is the guided mediation which can vary in length from five minutes to half an hour or more. It focuses the mind on one internal or external observation and helps reduce blood pressure, relax muscles and improve digestion. It clears the mind of unwanted thoughts both during the session, and for a significant length of time following it. For the best results use a guided mediation in the morning when the mind is more alert and better able to focus.   Though you can achieve good results in the evening, this is usually limited to improving sleep.

The five minute guided relaxation is becoming very popular and certainly gives you some of the benefits of a longer session.   These five minute sessions are popular on video streaming sites where they can be listened to for free.   Just make sure that nothing needs your attention while you listen, and for the best results sit or lie down with your head supported.

Retreats: These offer a way to spend time away from everyday life and give you a quiet space for inner reflection and meditation.   They can vary in their length from one day to two weeks or more, and many have different topics and themes.   There are probably retreat centres on your doorstep that you didn't even know existed.   Indeed I've lived here for twelve years and didn't realise there was an amazing centre just fifteen minutes walk away, set in acres of woodland with views of the local hills.

If you are struggling to identify who is the real you and want to remove all the external trappings of your everyday existence, the retreat can provide a valuable way to rediscover yourself and reconnect with your innermost self. Most retreat centres include private accommodation, meals, talks and group activities, but there are other working retreats where the aims and values of the retreat centre are practically discussed and teach the students how to live in harmony with nature and each other.

Learn to have fun: Surround yourself with what makes you happy and people who want the very best for you. Strive to do whatever you enjoy and view the world as your personal playground. Your broken inner child deserves the very best of everything it is possible to grant it without breaking the bank.

Learn to take pleasure in the smallest of things. Learn to appreciate all the small little details that adults take for granted and act too grown up to even notice. Learn to make even the most boring of household jobs a fun experience. You can learn to have the most amazing perspective on life if you learn to incorporate fun into everything you do. Put on some dance music to wash the pots to, take up trampolining, stop walking the dog and run with it instead, there are so many innovative ways to turn the mundane into the truly fantastic.

Rewriting Destiny:

You may have to live 'with' what happened in your past, but you don't have to live 'in it'. Reflect on what is, instead of what was. You can move on and distance yourself from it with each and every breakthrough. Don't let the abuse define you, you can have a great life. Learn that you can be loved and learn to see the negative patterns for what they are so you can let them go.

I just stopped talking about my parents and began again. Though it was their choice that I was detached from them, I learned to create a good place as the foundation of my new life and rewrote my own destiny through developing the right mindset.

It is not enough to just understand what happened and think that things will get better. There is history, and there is emotion invested in that history at a point in your life where the very fabric of your mind was being shaped and moulded. But today is the first day of the rest of your life, and there are many more days yet to come. Don't be the person who always talks about what their parents did to them when they were growing up, and how they messed you up. Usually no one wants to hear that, but more importantly you don't want to hear it either, you don't want to say it and you don't want to think it. If you must talk about it, at least speak to a professional.

The words that were spoken to you caused you damage, they reside in your subconscious and repeating them verbally or dwelling on them in conscious thought is a sure fire way to stay stuck in the past.

Nor is it enough to simply separate yourself from the abusers. Separation did nothing to heal my wounds at anything other than a snail's pace until I learned to mentally distance myself from them and the words that they used to label and abuse me. We are all individuals and our experiences and situations are different, but even when my father died the wounds of my past still bled, so physical separation alone is simply not enough.

Remember that children play, they laugh, they are physically active. They love to learn and explore. If you were missing this carefree period of your life when all you knew should have been love and fun, then rediscover it now. Change your environment, change your mind and pick up where you left off.

If your parents didn't let you grow and develop into the person you were meant to be, into the authentic you then you will not have naturally developed a healthy mindset. They interfered with your development, they broke and forced you into something else that is not you. You must carry on, get over what you didn't get and find out who you are and not who they said you were, either directly or indirectly. Now you are the adult you can acknowledge that you didn't get what you should have, but you can seek therapy, read up, get a life coach if needs be and learn to identify yourself in a new and healthy way.

Factory Reset -

Concept and Implementation:

Is it possible to undo the damage of the past? This is the question I sought to answer.

This chapter is dedicated to the route I took to reverse the ingrained toxicity that years of verbal and emotional abuse had cultivated in my mind. This chapter has been included as the conclusion of my life's struggle with this pain and the effect it has had on my day to day life. In all my years I had tried to look for ways to feel better, but initially I wasn't fully aware of why I felt so bad in the first place.

After an acknowledgement of the past abuse and the revelation of how my current fears were rooted in the lies I had been telling myself since childhood, I took a pragmatic approach to reverse the emotional lies.

The Inner Voice:

If your past experience has taught you to be closed, self conscious and self critical from a young age, it can be difficult to unlearn something that has effectively become hard wired into the brain almost from its conception. The first lesson to be learned is that of patience, and as you learn to give yourself patience, you also learn to give it freely to others in the process.

If love was given conditionally you may have learned to seek approval from other people, you may have learned to place the opinions of others ahead of your own in order to appease them. You will have learnt to constantly check that you are making them happy, lest you suffer the consequences. This constant need to approval must be unlearned.

If each time you opened up when you were younger and were either ridiculed, humiliated or punished you will have learnt to be closed and to keep even the most trivial of matters close to your chest. You will have learnt to build walls to protect yourself from harm, and may well be out of balance in this area.

If you are addicted to approval, if you believe that everyone else's opinion is better or more important than your own, then this must be unlearnt. All the little voices in your head that constantly speak ill of you and to you, the words that were either spoken to you by your parents, or that you spoke to yourself because of how you were treated need to be replaced with something better.

If you spend enough time repeating negative thoughts about yourself it becomes ingrained into your subconscious and you start to believe the thoughts to be a true reflection of reality. This then becomes a global belief, it taints your thoughts and changes the way you view yourself, who you are and what you are about.

If you hit a bad period later in your life, you know that your life wasn't always this way and can see the possibility that you might well see your way out of it someday. You might feel that you have failed at something, but know that you yourself are not a failure. This isn't the case when the negative thoughts or situation started from a young age. You never knew any other way, you never saw yourself as once happy and confident, or loved. You didn't see yourself differently at one time.

This can set the tone for the rest of your life unless you take action to address it and reverse the bad programming.

Reprogramming the Mind:

Perhaps it is because of my background in computers that I tend to view the mind as a piece of software and the brain and body as the hardware, however you perceive it the principle is the same. What was learnt must be unlearnt, and the self depreciating negative opinions that you have repeated over and over must be broken if you are ever to see yourself in a different light and move forward.

Take obesity for example. This typically occurs due to a consistent calorie intake which exceeds the bodies capacity to burn it off. It doesn't suddenly happen because someone once ate a cake, or ate a large portion of potato chips, it happens when someone is consistent in their overeating. To reverse the situation it will take more than one day of doing the right thing. A consistent action brought the person to the point they now find themselves in, and it will take a consistent action to bring them back out of it.

If someone consistently said damaging things to you, or you were treated in a consistent way that caused you to believe you were inferior, to halt the damage and beat it into remission it will take a repeated pattern that is its polar opposite.

This means replacing the negative belief system with a positive one.

'**I'm worthless**' must become '**I am worthy**'.

'**I just give up**' must be replaced with '**I cannot give up**'.

'No one wants to be around me' becomes **'what new person am I going to meet today'**.

'My life is a miserable mess' is replaced with **'this situation will ultimately work out for my good'**.

You might think those thoughts are not be a true reflection of reality, but neither was it true that your life was a miserable mess, but you believe that it is, so it feels like it. To you, your life is a miserable mess, so the desire to see anything more positive is hidden from your view. If you don't look for the good in a situation, you won't be drawn to it, immerse yourself in it or encourage it into reality.

If you ever meet someone who is outrageously positive, they would say their life is wonderful, that they feel so lucky, they have everything they need. Their thoughts are their reality, just as yours are to you. Something bad happens to them, yet they are unphased. Their mind is conditioned to look for the positive, they are drawn to the most smallest of success and they revel in it, they exist in it, they nurture it and they flourish because of it.

Like draws like, and the mind does not like to be proven wrong. You will look for any confirmation that your opinion is a valid one and disregard all the signs that prove otherwise.

The thoughts of the damaged mind should always be questioned, least of all trusted as always stating the truth. This mindset is not the most reliable sources of information, and its negative perspective might not provide the most balanced of views on which to base our situation.

So how is this achieved? How can you condition the mind from the negative to the positive? I have found that a two pronged approach achieves the most dramatic results. These steps are best taken each morning, but can also be repeated at night.

Stage 1 - Silence the Critic:

The inner voice speaks to us all times of the day and night. It chatters away, commenting and giving opinions on everything we say, see, think or do. We must learn to silence this inner voice before we can replace it with a more positive commentary. This first stage is rapidly achieved with a guided meditation session, which can be a free five minute video you can obtain from your favourite video sharing website or as a purchased audio download.

There are other types of meditation and of differing lengths of time to suit your schedule and personal preference, but their purpose is the same. This first stage will leave you feeling rested, relaxed and neutral minded. It will remove the anxiety and tension, but most of all it will silence the inner voices. This leaves you in the perfect mindset for the next stage.

Stage 2 - Replace the Pattern:

Following the meditation session after the inner critic has been suppressed, spend the next few minutes setting a new tone for the day. All the negative mindsets must be replaced with positive ones. These are the lessons we should have been taught as children, the words that should have become the foundation of our global beliefs of how we view ourselves and our place in the world. The beliefs that were denied us by those that should have taught it to us.

The second stage is achieved with a series of statements that we either quietly read to ourselves, or say aloud to cement words of encouragement, love and acceptance into our minds. These must positively cultivate the three cornerstones of our basic needs, and they are love, security and significance.

Commonly referred to as affirmations, these words will imprint themselves in our mind whilst still in a state of relaxation and neutrality. When repeated, they condition our minds to believe they are true, and in essence they subconsciously begin to change the way we feel about ourselves and how we view the situations of the day.

As our thoughts shape our reality, day by day these subtle changes begin to tell us new truths about who we are and how we should view ourselves. If we had been treated right, then we would have grown to become a self assured person with a positive inner monologue that supports and directs us into our adult life, instead of it becoming a negatron of self depreciation that constantly looks for evidence of our failures and slowly tears us apart.

You must do this every day until you cease to see yourself as a victim or the prisoner of your current mindset, and instead begin to see yourself as the person of worth and value that you are. A strong resilient character who has weathered an enormous storm and come through the other side to live another day. You are a true survivor in every sense, and the role model to your broken inner child.

These two actions will begin to silence the critical inner voice and replace it with the positive self affirming phrases that every healthy mind should carry with them from day to day. These are motivational phrases that will inspire you into action, give you a sense of hope and achievement, and begin to foster a sense of self-worth that was previously denied.

I would add that it's probably best to distance yourself from sources that could counteract or slow the attempt to undo the process. This might mean temporally separating yourself or restricting contact with the original source of the abuse which caused the issue, or similar situations which are helping to reinforce it.

If this means severing complete contact to protect your self interests then feel no sense of guilt. People may say that you owe your parents, but do not allow your nice nature to be influenced by the opinions of others.

While you were being abused they were not doing what was in your best interests, at best they wanted 'their version' of it. Do not allow yourself to be taken advantage of. Create your own space, get yourself in a good place where you can begin to undo the damage of the past, and enter a state of recovery. When you do find yourself in a better place, an amazing thing begins to happen. Instead of placing your self worth in other things and other people, you can draw it from your own sense of inner peace and value. From this new solid foundation you can begin to build renewed relationships with those closest to you.

You often hear people referring to someone they know as 'their rock', a solid immovable mountain of security. The person who radiates a quiet self assurance that has more than enough strength within themselves to be able to give it to others in their times of need. This completely changes the dynamics of your existing and new relationships. People are naturally drawn to strong characters who are dependable. You can be that type of person once the ghosts of the past have been exercised for good. It is not only possible to put the past firmly in its place and begin to restore and draw out the character of the person who was suppressed by it, I believe it is also possible to develop into a stronger human being because of it.

Author's Conclusion:

Your own story may be different to mine, but remember two different people can have the same experiences and yet respond to them in completely different ways. This is not about comparing whether the abuse that someone suffered was worse or less, the damage that a person feels will be as unique as they are.

It was the words that were spoken, and those that were not spoken that played over and over in my conscious mind. It was like reliving the same painful experiences again and again. Those words taught me something, they taught me that I wasn't important, that I wasn't wanted and that I would never amount to anything. Given the power of those words that changed the direction of my life, I decided to choose new words that would change it again. When you learn to use these words on yourself, you can use them on others to empower them in return. At home, at work, or on complete strangers you just happen to get into a conversation with, you can choose the right words to uplift and encourage. We cannot erase memories, but we can re-write new ones instead of repeating the same old ones of the past.

Parents were once children too, and perhaps broken in the same way that we, the next casualty in what could have been a long line of hurting people were also damaged. It is up to each individual to reach a sense of acceptance and make their own way out of the pain in their own timing. For me, a combination of psychotherapy, natural conclusions and self help were enough to see myself in a different light and begin to reverse the damage of a troubled childhood.

If self help does not work for you, then please seek the advice of a certified professional who can work with you through your own issues and in your own time, because I believe that a person can take their damaged past, turn their back on it and begin to move in a new direction. I believe that a person can reclaim their self confidence and know what it is like to feel positive and secure. I also believe that a person can nurture this strength within themselves and begin to spread it to those around them in a way that someone who never knew what it was like to feel emotional pain could ever do.

I hope that if you identified with this story and the damage it caused, that you can also identify with the sense of hope. Thank you for taking the time to read this book, I wish you the very best for your own future, and hope that in sharing my own story, it can help you in some small way with yours.

Kind regards,

Chris Radford.

Bonus Material:

As meditation and affirmations have been so helpful in my own recovery, I have included the following resources which you might find helpful. You can use them in your own recovery process, or just to generally improve your state of mind as part of a morning routine.

What is Meditation?

This is a practice which helps to clear the mind of unwanted thoughts by focusing all conscious attention into one single point. It is used for (but not limited to) promoting a balanced state of mind, fostering relaxation, increasing a feeling of wellbeing, and encouragement of a non judgemental attitude. It can also be used to clear unwanted negative thoughts.

In psychotherapy it is used to help treat stress and depression and can dramatically reduce the symptoms associated with anxiety, including muscle tension and tension headaches.

There are many different methods of meditation including guided meditation and mindfulness meditation, and these can be found freely on video sharing and streaming platforms if you decide to take this route. They can also be purchased as audio downloads or hypnosis compact discs.

Three general exercises are included below for your convenience:

Basic Meditation Exercise:

1. Get into a comfortable position, either sitting or lying down is fine, but ensure that nothing needs your attention for the duration of the exercise.
2. Close your eyes or softly gaze.
3. Without making any attempt to change it, notice your breathing.
4. If your attention wanders, simply return to the breath.

5. Notice where the breath is felt strongest, this might be in your chest, or your belly.

6. Observe that the coolness of the in-breath is different to the warmth of the out-breath.

7. See if you can notice one complete breath from beginning to end.

8. Imagine that with each out-breath you are breathing out tension, and with each in-breath you are breathing in calmness.

9. Maintain this attention for at least a few minutes unless you begin to feel a sense of calm.

10. When you are ready to finish, simply open your eyes, wiggle your toes, have a good stretch, and continue with the rest of your day.

Basic Progressive Muscle Relaxation:

1. Get into a comfortable position, either sitting or lying down is fine, but ensure that nothing

needs your attention for the duration of the exercise.

2.   Close your eyes or softly gaze.

3.   Place your hands comfortably on your lap, or if you are lying down place your hands by your sides.

4.   Clench both your hands into fists, holding them tightly in this position, but not so tightly as to cause too much discomfort.

5.   Notice how tight and restricted the hands feel, notice the tension in the fingers.

6.   Now release the hands and let the fingers feel free, and notice how much more comfortable this feels compared to the tension that was there before.

7.   You might begin to notice a warm feeling in your fingers, like gentle ripples of energy.

8.   Focus your attention on your hands and the relaxed sensation you now feel.

9.   If your attention wanders, simply return your focus to the hands.

10. Keeping your hands relaxed, now tense the forearms, pulling them tightly but not so tightly as to cause too much discomfort.

11. Notice how tight and tense the forearms feel.

12. Now release the tension and let your arms feel free and loose, and notice how much more comfortable this feels compared to the tension that was there before.

13. Notice the pleasant feeling of warm energy that now flows from your finger tips to your elbows.

14. Focus your attention on your lower arms and the relaxed sensation you now feel.

15. If you wish, repeat the same process with your upper arms, and in turn with other areas of the body until you feel relaxation from the tips of your toes to the top of your head.

16. When you are ready to finish, simply open your eyes, wiggle your toes, have a good stretch, and continue with the rest of your day.

Basic Counting Meditation:

1. Get into a comfortable position, either sitting or lying down is fine, but ensure that nothing needs your attention for the duration of the exercise.

2. Close your eyes or softly gaze.

3. Without making any attempt to change it, notice your breathing.

4. If your attention wanders, simply return to the breath.

5. On the next out breath, imagine that you are breathing out tension, imagine it as a grey mist and think the number 10 as you do.

6. Breathe in calmness.

7. On the next out breath, imagine that you are breathing out even more old tension, imagine this as a grey mist and think the number 9.

8. Then breathe in calmness.

9. Repeat this process until you reach the number 0.

10. When you are ready to finish, simply open your eyes, wiggle your toes, have a good stretch, and continue with the rest of your day.

You can vary the length of these meditations to suit your own stress levels or available time constraints. You can also use them two or three times per day if you wish, but for maximum effect use them at the start of the day when the mind is most able to focus.

Directing the mind at the beginning of the day sets you up for an amazing and productive experience in the hours that follow. Meditation calms, relaxes and builds resistance against stress.

What are Affirmations?

Most people repeat the same affirmations to themselves every day without realising it, but they are often from the self critical and unhelpful inner monologue that chatters away to our subconscious every waking moment. These negative affirmations are usually made up of labels that people have given us in the past, or how we view ourselves and what we have achieved. Very often they make us feel bad about ourselves and compare our achievements to those of others, so even our best progress can be tainted with negativity.

Positive affirmations are difficult to read at first because they can often seem like lies or that we are fooling ourselves, but our negative inner monologue does the exact same thing, except in reverse. We have grown so accustomed to critical thoughts, that at first positive affirmations are difficult to accept, but they are a powerful tool in reshaping the way we see and think of ourselves and what we have achieved. Like draws like, and by accepting these new affirmations, they can become self fulfilling prophetic statements that do far more than rapidly change your state, they can change the destiny of your life and usher you into a fantastic new way of living. It's time to unlearn everything that you have been taught about hate.

A New Day:

Today is a great day, and it will be a day to remember.

I greet every new day with wonder and excitement.

The past is behind me, my future is before me.

I never know what amazing new person I will meet today.

I am unique, I am one of a kind, I am blessed and I am more than enough.

I am in control of how I feel, and today I feel fantastic.

I treat myself with the love, patience and kindness that I truly deserve.

I am a money magnet, I attract financial resources.

I have more than enough joy and love to share with myself and others.

I compare myself to no one but my own sense of achievement.

Every day is beautiful and I greet it as though it were my very first.

I treat everyone I meet with kindness and with dignity, and I receive it in return.

I am a wonderful gift to the world, and also to myself.

Good things come easily to me, I attract health, wealth and happiness.

My happiness brings me happy things and happy people.

I am skilled in financial management, and make good financial decisions.

My life is the stuff of dreams.

I am in charge of how I feel, and today I choose to be happy.

I am one of a kind, and I am free to be the real me.

My determination to succeed and not give up makes me awesome and amazing.

I am a miracle of life.

I see the possibilities in every situation.

Money comes to me effortlessly and easily.

I see the good in others, and also in myself.

Today I am excited... about everything.

Dreams and Goals:

Now is not the time to give up on my goals.

I shall not give up until I have tried every possible way to succeed.

I choose to follow my dreams no matter how things may appear.

I am in charge of my own mind, and the possibilities are endless.

I gain strength from my past because I am simply awesome.

I love what I do, I am good at it and it comes easily to me.

I make good smart decisions about my future.

I regret nothing, my future is bright and full of opportunity.

My reality is based on my thoughts, so I plan a fantastic day that is full of joy.

If I see it in my mind, it will become mine to hold in my hand.

Facing Problems:

I am resourceful and I have the ability to get through any situation.

All problems have a solution, and this one is no different.

I accept my mistakes, I learn from them, and I flourish.

I effortlessly let go of fear and pain, and I replace them with goals and energy.

I am bigger than any problem that lies before me.

A solution will present itself in due time, and when it does I will act upon it.

I will delay giving up for just one more day.

I know this situation will ultimately lead to something truly amazing.

I can handle anything that comes my way with dignity and peace.

A cloud is not the sky, I count my blessings, not the curses.

Love and Relationships:

I am happy, I am loveable and I am totally wonderful.

Anyone would be extremely lucky and fortunate to have me in their life.

I am more than willing and able to start a brand new chapter.

I am healthy, attractive and worthy.

I have a blessed life, filled with wonderful people.

It will happen at the right time and for the right reasons.

I am worth it.

My life is beautiful, and I am worthy of true love.

People see me as I am - incredible, capable and confident.

I naturally attract kindness and love.

The love I give to others will be returned to me.

I am ready to accept a loving, caring and healthy relationship.

Diet and Weight Loss:

My self worth is not based upon my weight, or my waistline measurement.

I eat only the foods that are nutritious, healthy and taste great.

Losing weight comes naturally to me, and it is fun.

Every day I feel fitter, look slimmer and grow stronger.

I believe in myself, and my ability to change anything I put my mind to.

My setbacks only make me more determined to succeed.

Exercise makes me feel great.

I have the power to create a real change in my life.

My goals are more important than the contents of my fridge.

I am beautiful, and even my flaws have their own sense of charm.

Today is a new day and I begin again.

I take good care of my body and treat it with the dignity and respect it deserves.

I have already succeeded, and my actions today will prove that to be true.

You can easily create your own affirmations, and even write some of them down and place them around the house to keep you going throughout the day. To write the most powerful affirmations consider using bold words for maximum impact, for example, 'exercise makes me feel good' could be 'exercise makes me feel great' or 'this will lead to something good' could be 'this will lead to something truly amazing'.

Affirmations are a great way to start your day, with lifestyle gurus and motivational speakers all seemingly tapping into the powerful state that can be achieved when using them to great effect at the start of the day.

Make no mistake, words carry tremendous power. With words alone treaties can be formed, empires can be built and lifelong friendships forged. They can start wars and can even end them when all hope for peace was seemingly lost.

Words alone can break the spirit of the youngest and happiest healthy mind, and words have the power to restore and heal it.

If you believe that words spoken to you in your most impressionable and vulnerable years have made you the person you are today, then believe that words spoken to you now can mend, restore and reshape you into the person you truly want to be. You already know their power, you have lived under their curse for all your life, echoes of the subconscious have whispered their lies to you. They have shaped your destiny, and led you to this very point in time. They are containers for power and possibly the single most powerful force available to humanity.

Now you know their power, now you know what they can achieve, what will you do with them? How will you use them? Where will they take you? And how will you use them to shape your own life, and the lives of those around you?

Kind regards,

Chris Radford.

Made in the USA
San Bernardino, CA
20 November 2018